W9-BKA-474

Spy Technology

Ron Fridell

LERNER PUBLICATIONS COMPANY
MINNEAPOLIS

Lerner Publications Company
A division of Lerner Publishing Group
241 First Avenue North
Minneapolis, Minnesota 55401 U.S.A.

Website address: www.lernerbooks.com

Library of Congress Cataloging-in-Publication Data

Fridell, Ron.
    Spy technology / by Ron Fridell.
        p.   cm. — (Cool science)
    Includes bibliographical references and index.
    ISBN-13: 978–0-8225–5934–4 (lib. bdg. : alk. paper)
    ISBN-10: 0–8225–5934–X (lib. bdg. : alk. paper)
    1. Espionage—Technological innovations—Juvenile literature.   I. Title.   II. Series.
  UB270.5.F75 2007
  623'.71—dc22   2005033043

Manufactured in the United States of America
1 2 3 4 5 6 – BP – 12 11 10 09 08 07

Table of Contents

Introduction · · · · · · · · · · · · · · · 4

chapter 1 · · · · · · · · · · · · · · · · · 6
Spy Tech That Watches

chapter 2 · · · · · · · · · · · · · · · · 14
Spy Tech That Listens

chapter 3 · · · · · · · · · · · · · · · · 22
Secret Messages

chapter 4 · · · · · · · · · · · · · · · · 30
Dangerous Missions

chapter 5 · · · · · · · · · · · · · · · · 38
Future Spy Tech

Glossary · · · · · · · · · · · · · · · · · 44
Selected Bibliography · · · · · · · · · · 45
Further Reading and Websites · · · · 45
Index · · · · · · · · · · · · · · · · · · · 47

Introduction

Can you think fast? Can you keep a secret? Are you daring? Then you might make a good spy. Spies steal secrets for a living.

Stealing secrets is a very old job. Spies from Europe set out to steal a precious secret from China about 1,500 years ago. At that time, the Chinese were making beautiful silk fabric. They created it from the cocoons of silkworms. No one else knew how to make it.

IT'S A FACT!

A silkworm needs three to five days to spin its cocoon.

The spies disguised themselves as holy men. They carried canes with hollow ends. That's where they hid silkworm eggs they stole in China. Later, back in Europe, the eggs hatched into silkworm caterpillars, which then spun cocoons. Europe had captured the secret of silk making.

For many years, only the Chinese knew how to turn silkworm cocoons (above) into silk. Spies from Europe stole this secret about 1,500 years ago.

Hollowed-out canes were the simple spy technology of long ago. Modern spies use more complex tools. They can see in the dark with night vision goggles. Satellites in outer space show them close-up views of missile sites. Laser microphones let them hear top secret conversations. All around the world, spy tech lets spies watch and listen for secrets.

Spy Tech That Watches

The information that spies gather is called intelligence. When this intelligence comes in the form of pictures, it's known as IMINT: IMage INTelligence.

Sneakies is another spy term. These are the tools spies use to gather intelligence. Some sneakies are tiny cameras. The camera lens may look out through a hole in a wall, down from a light fixture, or up from a heating vent.

Some spies carry secret cameras too. A camera might be hidden in the frames of a spy's glasses, in a wristwatch, or in a shirt button.

This Japanese spy camera looks like a lighter.

6

A thin wire runs from the hidden camera to the spy's pocket. By pressing on the wire's end—click!—the spy snaps a secret picture.

Cold War Spies

Spies used sneakies like these during the Cold War years. Those were the years between the end of World War II in 1945 and the 1991 breakup of the Union of Soviet Socialist Republics (USSR), also known as the Soviet Union. This war was "cold" because no actual battles were fought. Instead, the United States and the Soviet Union stole secrets from each other.

The Soviet Union had a Communist government. It wanted more countries to become Communist. U.S. leaders saw Communism as a threat to the United States. They wanted to stop Communism from spreading.

On the U.S. side, the Central Intelligence Agency (CIA) had the job of finding out what the Soviet Union was up to. CIA agents spy on other nations. The Soviet spy agency was the KGB. Both agencies developed all sorts of sneakies to use in the spying game.

The U.S. government keeps most of its recent information about spying secret. But a lot is known about Cold War spy technology. The Cold War years were the golden age of spying. More spies did more spying with more clever and unusual kinds of gadgets during the Cold War than ever, before or since.

Night Vision

Imagine watching someone standing 200 yards (183 meters) away on a cloudy, moonless night. Impossible? Not if you have a high-quality night vision device (NVD). Your NVD could be a camera, binoculars, or goggles. Everything will appear in shades of green, but your view will be clear and sharp.

How does night vision work? Let's say you're a spy on a hilltop. Your mission is to photograph another nation's top secret missile site, 100 yards (90 m) below. You train your night vision camera on the site. What do you see?

Even in a remote spot on a dark night, there is some light from the stars and from distant cities. Your NVD lens captures this low-level light and sends it through a tube. The light is in the form of photons, which are particles of light energy. At the back of the tube is a screen of phosphors. These chemicals give off a greenish light. The tube shoots the incoming photons onto the phosphor screen. The screen multiplies them thousands of times. More photons mean more light. Now the greenish image is visible to your eye and bright enough to produce a clear picture.

Who Spies and Why

Spies usually work for secret agencies. In the United States, the National Security Agency (NSA) is the most secret secret agency of all. One of the NSA's jobs is to analyze intelligence that other agencies gather. It also monitors telephone calls and e-mail messages for signs of terrorism. In certain cases, it can spy on U.S. citizens.

The U.S. Central Intelligence Agency (CIA) gathers secret intelligence in foreign nations. Some U.S. government employees in foreign countries are really CIA spies working undercover. CIA spies look for military and economic secrets.

The Federal Bureau of Investigation (FBI) hunts for enemy spies in the United States. FBI agents also hunt for terrorists and other criminals.

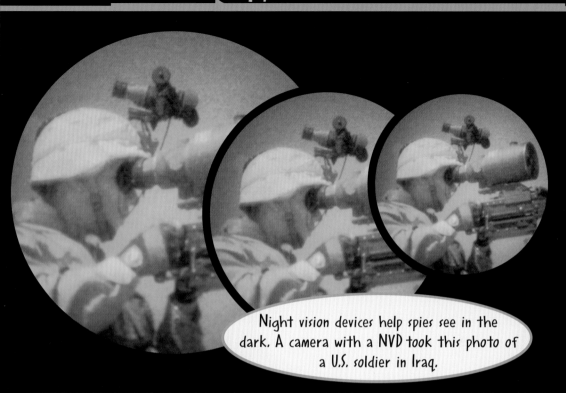

Night vision devices help spies see in the dark. A camera with a NVD took this photo of a U.S. soldier in Iraq.

Spies aren't the only people who use NVDs. Pilots and soldiers use night vision binoculars and goggles. You can even buy your own NVD in camera stores and over the Internet.

Sky Spies

Spy planes use powerful cameras to photograph secret missile sites and enemy soldiers far beneath them. People began using spy planes in World War I (1914–1918). During the Cold War, each side raced to produce spy planes that flew higher while getting sharper, closer images of things on the ground. The U.S. U-2 spy plane could snap sharp images from more than 13 miles (21 kilometers) up.

But spy planes can be shot down. In 1960, a Soviet missile knocked a U-2 out of the sky. The U.S. pilot, Francis Gary Powers, was lucky to survive after parachuting to Earth. The Soviets captured Powers but later returned him to the United States unharmed.

Pilot Francis Gary Powers (right) flew the U-2 spy plane (above). In 1960, he was shot down while on a spy mission over the Soviet Union.

The military wanted spy planes that could gather IMINT without risking human life. So engineers designed unmanned aerial vehicles (UAVs). These small, pilotless planes are guided by remote control.

The latest UAVs can fly at altitudes of 10 miles (16 km). These amazing machines send back images that show areas as small as 1 square foot (0.09 sq. m) in sharp detail. They include DarkStar, Global Hawk, and Predator. UAVs can also carry weapons. In 2002, in the Middle Eastern nation of Yemen, a Predator dropped a Hellfire missile on a vehicle carrying suspected terrorists.

Eyes in Outer Space

The Cold War eventually reached all the way to outer space. In 1960, the United States launched the first successful spy satellite,

Operation Pigeon

Some of the CIA's Cold War sneakies worked. Others did not. One failure featured a pigeon. CIA agents created a minicamera that fit around the bird's neck. When the pigeon turned its head, the camera snapped a picture. Agents trained a pigeon to work the camera. Then they turned it loose in Washington, D.C., for a test run.

The pigeon was supposed to fly around the city and snap a few pictures, then fly right back. But the pigeon didn't return on time. Instead, the pigeon came back to the launch site two days later— on foot! The camera was too heavy. The bird could fly only a short distance and then had to walk. Operation Pigeon never got off the ground.

Many nations have tried using pigeons as spies. French officials attached cameras to pigeons as early as 1910 (right).

Discoverer 14. It orbited Earth seven times and took pictures. Then it splashed down in the Pacific Ocean near Hawaii. On its way down, *Discoverer* ejected a capsule with parachutes attached. The capsule was plucked from midair by a specially equipped U.S. Air Force plane. Inside the capsule was film with valuable images of Soviet air bases and missile sites.

This plane is carrying a package of images from the first U.S. spy satellite.

In 1976, the United States launched the first spy satellite that could take pictures without film. It beamed the images straight down to Earth in digital data streams. Technicians on the ground could watch live images from the satellite.

The key to this new spy tech was silicon chips. These miniature electronic devices also help run computers. In satellites, the chips transform the visible light from the view below into electrical charges. These charges are beamed down to a receiving station on Earth. At the station, computers change the data streams back into visible images.

IMINT for Peace

As every spy knows, the world can be a very dangerous place. IMINT from spy satellites can help us watch for danger. In July 1995, a U.S. satellite beamed down images from the Eastern European nation of Bosnia-Herzegovina. Bosnia-Herzegovina was the site of a brutal civil war in the 1990s. The United States and other nations were trying to bring peace to the region.

The U.S. satellite images showed several hundred men held prisoner at a soccer field. A few days later, a U-2 spy plane flew over the same area. The images showed no prisoners. But there were signs that a mass grave had been dug in the field.

Experts said the IMINT proved that the prisoners had been killed and buried by their captors. This massacre outraged people worldwide. Something had to be done to stop the fighting. That same year, peace talks took place in Dayton, Ohio. The Dayton Peace Accords put an end to the civil war.

A U-2 spy plane took this photo in 1995 of land in Bosnia-Herzegovina. The arrows show where prisoners had been buried in a mass grave.

Recently disturbed earth

Unclassified

Chapter 2

Spy Tech That Listens

When intelligence comes in the form of messages, it's called COMINT—COMmunications INTelligence. Most COMINT is carried by radio waves. If radio waves weren't invisible, you could see thousands of them flying by your head in all directions. Cell phones work by radio waves. So do television and radio broadcasts, and some e-mail.

Spy tech bugs also use radio waves. A bug has two main parts, a mini microphone and a tiny radio transmitter. The microphone picks up sounds, and the transmitter sends them to headphones or

Spies plant listening devices, or bugs, out of sight.

a tape recorder. Like spy cameras, bugs can be hidden almost any-where. During the Cold War, some CIA agents wore bugged wrist-watches. A thin wire ran from the watch to a mini tape recorder under the agent's clothing.

Another Cold War bug looked like a twig. This twig was actually made of fiberglass. The CIA noticed that the Chinese ambassador often had private conversations on a certain park bench. CIA agents left the bugged twig next to the bench to pick up the ambassador's secrets.

Even shoes could hide Cold War bugs. A U.S. ambassador to Czechoslo-vakia ordered a pair of new shoes. The shoes would be delivered in the mail. When Czech spies found this out, they took the package from the post office and planted a bug in one of the heels. The ambassador's per-sonal servant was a Czech secret agent. He turned on the shoe bug whenever the U.S. ambassador went to a secret meeting.

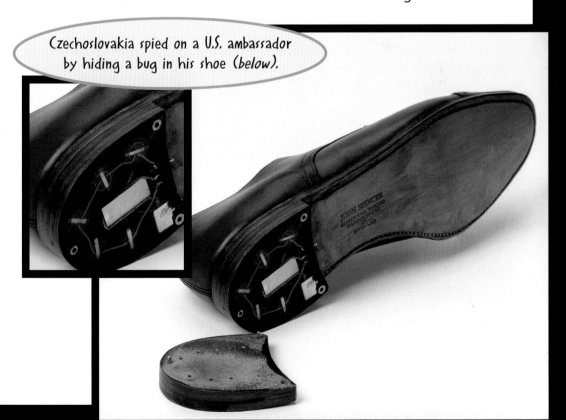

Czechoslovakia spied on a U.S. ambassador by hiding a bug in his shoe (below).

Eavesdropping

Eavesdropping is a word linked to spying. It comes from eaves—the lower edge of the roof that hangs out away from the house. This wide overhang of eaves keeps rain safely away. But it also gives spies a dark, sheltered place to hide outside and eavesdrop—listen in on secret conversations inside the house.

All these Cold War sneakies could make North Americans and Soviets suspicious of one another. In 1972, a Canadian hockey team traveled to Moscow, Russia, to play a Soviet team. The Canadian players suspected the Soviets had bugged their hotel rooms.

One night, two players searched their room. They checked everything from the light fixture on the ceiling to the rugs on the floor, looking for hidden microphones. They found nothing suspicious until they pulled back the rug. There on the floor was a round piece of metal.

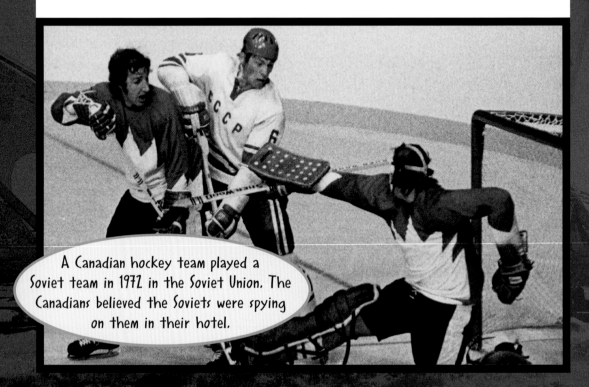

A Canadian hockey team played a Soviet team in 1972 in the Soviet Union. The Canadians believed the Soviets were spying on them in their hotel.

The players figured they'd found a bug, so they worked on getting rid of it. They unscrewed the metal piece and pulled. A moment later, they felt a hard tug and heard a crashing sound. The round piece of metal was not a bug after all. It had held up the light fixture in the room below. The crash was the fixture hitting the floor.

Spies and Counterspies

Modern spies pick up conversations without using bugs. They use laser microphones instead. These high-tech listening devices shoot laser beams to distant windows. The voices of the people inside make the window glass vibrate slightly. The laser hits the glass and bounces back. Each word a person speaks makes a slightly different vibration. The laser device picks up the tiny differences in vibration and turns them into words.

A Monstrosity!

One Cold War spy project was so weird that an ex-CIA officer calls it "a monstrosity!" It was known as Acoustic Kitty.

The CIA operated on a normal male cat. They installed batteries and a bug inside him. His tail was the antenna. Acoustic Kitty could pick up conversations between spies.

The hard part was training the cat to walk to a certain spot and stay there. Finally, agents decided he was ready for his first mission. They put him in a van, along with listening and recording equipment, and drove him to a park. Across the street, two men sat on a park bench talking.

CIA agents opened the van door and pointed the cat toward the bench. Then they let him go. Moments later, a taxi ran him over. That was the sad end of Acoustic Kitty.

Stealing secrets is one part of spying. The other part is counterspying: protecting your nation's secrets from foreign spies. That's why so many government buildings have thick fabric curtains across the windows. The curtains absorb the sounds of conversations before they can get to the window glass. That helps keep the secrets safe.

Bugs can be countered as well. Agents use a device called a broom to "sweep" buildings for bugs. The broom broadcasts a radio signal that makes any bugs nearby give off signals of their own. Then agents can disable (take apart) the bugs.

Internet Spies

Millions of people—including criminals—use e-mail to send messages by computer. The FBI spies on criminals in the United States. Since terrorists, drug traffickers, and other serious criminals use e-mail, so do FBI agents.

The FBI and other spy agencies check e-mail messages for tips about terrorist attacks.

Congress passed the USA Patriot Act in 2001. The act is a series of laws. One of these laws, known as Section 212, gives FBI agents access to private e-mails.

All e-mail messages use an Internet service provider (ISP). An ISP is like a post office. Messages must pass through it on their way from the sender to the receiver. Before the Patriot Act, the FBI could look at certain e-mails from an ISP after getting permission from a court. This can take anywhere from hours to days.

IT'S A FACT!
Worldwide, there are more than 684 million e-mail users.

Section 212 expands the FBI's power when lives are at risk. In those cases, agents may look at e-mails without court permission.

For example, in 2004, someone sent an e-mail threatening to burn down a mosque, an Islamic place of worship, in El Paso, Texas. When FBI agents got a tip about the e-mail, they asked the ISP to give it to them. The ISP agreed. Agents quickly traced the e-mail back to its sender before he could carry out his threat.

Some lawmakers do not like Section 212. They think it gives the FBI too much spying power. They worry that the FBI can spy on anyone at any time.

Ears in Outer Space

Earth curves, but radio signals travel in straight lines. That's why cell phone towers and other signal stations are set up all around the world. These stations pick up radio signals before they fly off into space and

Spy agencies have tools that let them listen in on cell phone conversations.

redirect them to the next station. That's how a person in Alaska can call a friend in Brazil. Dozens of stations keep the cell phone signal moving ahead along Earth's curving surface from city to city.

What does this have to do with spying? A station picks up only a little of the signal. That's all it needs to pass on to the next station. The unused part of the signal flies out over the horizon into outer space, where spy satellites can pick it up.

This is true of each of the billions of messages sent by radio waves on any given day anywhere in the world. This includes cell phone calls, ground line phone calls, faxes, e-mail messages, and more.

Project Echelon

The United States and four other nations run a top secret spy satellite network called Echelon. Experts say Echelon can intercept (pick up) any message sent by radio waves anywhere in the world. It probably picks up hundreds of millions of messages each day. The messages go to NSA headquarters in Fort Meade, Maryland.

IT'S A FACT!
Some people say the NSA is so secret that the initials should stand for "Never Say Anything."

There, supercomputers scan each message the way search engines scan the Internet. They look for certain words and phrases, such as names of known terrorists, from a watch list that is updated daily. Whenever the computers spot a word from the watch list, they save the message.

The saved messages go to NSA agents. They analyze this intelligence every day. Sometimes you might hear news broadcasts warning of a possible terrorist attack. The newscaster may say that the government has noticed "increased levels of chatter" from terrorists. This "chatter" probably comes from messages picked up by Echelon spy satellites.

The NSA has its headquarters in Fort Meade, Maryland (above). The number of employees working for the NSA is classified.

chapter 5

Secret Messages

Every good spy knows that secrets must travel in secret. The enemy can't know that you know their secrets. Your secret message could be intercepted. The enemy must not be able to figure out what the message means.

So spies turn their secret intelligence into ciphers and codes. In a cipher, you replace each individual letter with another letter or a number. Ciphers work according to a plan known only to the sender and receiver. Let's say you're an army commander who receives this cipher message from one of your spies: **fofnz gpsdft ifbejoh gps pvs xftufso cpsefs**.

As commander, you know the key to the cipher. Each letter has been replaced with the letter in the alphabet that comes after it. The letter *f* stands for *e* and so on. What is your spy telling you?

IT'S A FACT!

Humans have used ciphers for more than two thousand years.

Answer: enemy forces heading for our western border

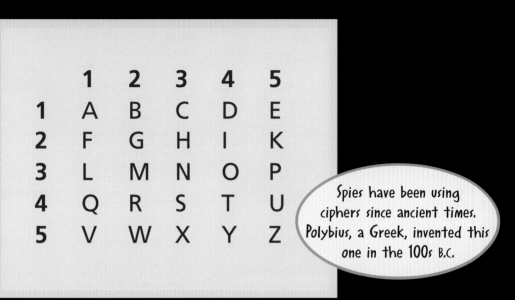

	1	2	3	4	5
1	A	B	C	D	E
2	F	G	H	I	K
3	L	M	N	O	P
4	Q	R	S	T	U
5	V	W	X	Y	Z

Spies have been using ciphers since ancient times. Polybius, a Greek, invented this one in the 100s B.C.

Another cipher is called the Polybius Square *(above)*. Notice that *J* is missing. The *J* has been combined with *I* so the grid comes out even, five rows across and five rows down. A word written in this cipher looks like this: **23-15-31-35**. Each letter is shown by its coordinates on the grid. The first number is from the column on the left. The second number is from the row along the top. So **23** stands for **H**. What is the word?

Thomas Jefferson was the third president of the United States. He also invented a cipher in the early 1790s. Jefferson's wheel cipher is made of twenty-six wooden disks on an iron axle. On the rim of each disk, the twenty-six letters of the alphabet appear in a different random order. The message sender and the receiver both have identical cipher wheels.

The sender turns the disks on the cipher wheel until one horizontal row spells out his message of twenty-six letters or less. The letters on the other rows don't spell anything. The sender writes down the letters of one of the nonsense rows and sends that message to the receiver.

Thomas Jefferson invented this wheel cipher in the early 1790s. It can spell out a message that is twenty-six letters long.

If anyone intercepts the nonsense message, that person will have no idea what the message says. Only the receiver can read the message. Here's how. She lines up one row of her wheel cipher to spell out the nonsense message. That means that somewhere on her wheel, the actual message is spelled out for her to read, just as it was on the sender's wheel.

A Spy's Note

Spies know that getting intelligence to the people who need it is tricky. Many things can go wrong along the way. During the American Revolution (1775–1783), soldiers fighting for the British were camped in Trenton, New Jersey. A spy arrived with a note for the commander. The commander was in the middle of a card game. He stuffed the note into his pocket to read later. The note warned that George Washington's army was headed toward the British camp.

If the commander had read the spy's note, his soldiers would have been prepared for the attack. But he forgot all about it. The Battle of Trenton was the first major victory for George Washington and his Continental army.

Cracking Codes

By the beginning of the twentieth century, spies had turned from ciphers to codes. In a code, words are replaced by groups of numbers or letters from a secret codebook. Here is part of a coded secret message known as the Zimmerman Telegram: **130 13042 13041 8501 115 3528 416**.

This message is from World War I. Germany and Britain were enemies in the war. Germany sent the message in 1917. Britain intercepted it. Codes are harder to figure out than ciphers. Without the secret codebook, you must use mathematical formulas to crack the code and figure out what it means.

When a British intelligence officer cracked the German code, the British sent the decoded Zimmerman Telegram to the United States. This move

The Navajo Code Talkers

During World War II (1939–1945), twenty-nine Native Americans helped the United States and its allies defeat Japan and win the war. This group was the Navajo code talkers. The Navajo Nation extends through Utah, New Mexico, and Arizona.

The code talkers were members of the U.S. Marine Corps. They created a code so difficult that the Japanese couldn't crack it. The key was the Navajo language. It was a spoken language only. Only a few non-Navajos knew it. And none of them were Japanese. The Navajo Marines wrote a dictionary of their language, using Navajo words to stand for military words. Besh-lo, for example, means "iron fish" in Navajo. In the new code, it meant "submarine."

How important was this work? A key battle was the one for the Japanese island of Iwo Jima. A U.S. marine leader said, "Were it not for the Navajos, the marines would never have taken Iwo Jima."

changed the course of history. The United States was not yet fighting in the war. But the decoded telegram said the Germans wanted Mexico to help them attack the United States. So the U.S. government declared war on Germany. The war ended in 1918 with Germany's defeat.

Secret Containers

Putting a message into code or cipher is not always enough to keep it secret. A spy in enemy territory may also have to carry the message safely back to the home country in a "sneaky" of some kind.

Spies are good at finding unexpected places to hide things. Secret messages have been hidden rolled up in walnut shells or inserted into artificial eyes. They have been written on the backs of stamps or tucked into shoe heels. Even a coin might contain a message.

During World War II, spies would hide an entire map in a deck of cards. Playing cards are made from two pieces of paper that have been stuck together. The spies would separate the two parts of the cards. Then

they would cut the map into tiny pieces and number each piece. They hid the map in the middle of the playing cards and stuck the cards back together. Later, the map pieces could be reassembled like a jigsaw puzzle.

This coin looks like a normal silver dollar. But it has a secret hiding place.

Even sticky tape can be a sneaky. A group of Soviet scientists toured a U.S. aircraft plant in 1983. The United States and the Soviet Union were enemies, but they would sometimes allow visits under carefully controlled conditions. The visiting Soviets were checked from head to toe to be sure they carried no spy cameras or listening devices.

No one checked their shoes, though. The Soviets had strips of sticky tape on the bottom of each shoe. As they walked through the plant, the tape picked up slivers of a secret metal alloy used in U.S. fighter planes.

Invisible Words

Steganography is a spy term for another way of hiding secret messages. The word is Greek for "covered writing." It's an old technique. In ancient times, a secret message would be tattooed on a messenger's bald head. Once his hair grew back, the messenger would be sent on his way.

Or the message might be written on the stomach of a rabbit that the messenger carried with him. Either way, the secret was safely hidden from view.

Using invisible ink is a great way to hide messages. Lemon juice or milk can be used as ink. A toothpick or a

Spies can use invisible ink to send messages. The ink reappears when the paper is held over a heat source.

fingertip becomes the pen. Once the liquid dries, the paper looks blank. When the paper is heated with an iron, an oven, or a 100-watt lightbulb, the message becomes visible.

Secret Specks

Look at the period at the end of this sentence. Imagine that it contains a secret message. It could. A microdot camera can shrink secret information to the size of a period.

Let's say you're a spy in a room full of secret documents in a foreign nation. You must know what's in the documents, but the enemy must not know you've got them. So instead of stealing the documents, you lay them on a desktop. Beside them, you make a pile of books 2 feet (0.6 m) high. You slide a plastic ruler with holes in it in between the top two books. You fit your microdot camera into a hole in the ruler, pointing

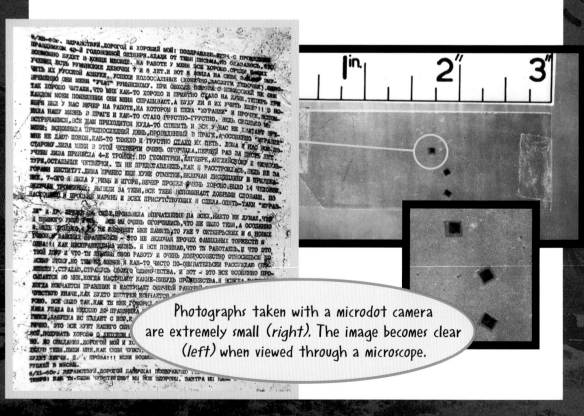

Photographs taken with a microdot camera are extremely small (*right*). The image becomes clear (*left*) when viewed through a microscope.

down at the documents. After photographing them, you put every-thing back where you found it and quietly slip away.

Back at your hotel, you remove the film from the camera, and all you see is a series of specks. Each one is a microdot, a microscopic image of one of the secret documents. You roll up the film and place it inside a tiny secret compartment in your ring.

Later, at the airport, you wait as your baggage is searched and you are patted down from head to toe. Then you step onto your plane and fly safely away. Back in your home country, other agents place the microdots under high-powered microscopes to view the secret documents.

Software Secrets

The scene above is from the Cold War days. Modern spies would prob-ably use computers to create, conceal, transmit, and view images of secret information. The key is pixels.

Each image on a TV or computer screen is made up of thousands of bits of information called pixels. Each pixel is a tiny part of the image. With special software, you can select only certain pixels to look at, while elim-inating the others. So with a few keystrokes, you can turn a picture of a farm field, say, into an image of a secret missile installation.

You can also hide a secret written message by putting it in the same color as the background on a computer screen. If this page were on a computer screen, for example, the secret message could be in white letters, invisible to the eye. The person who receives the message could then change the background color to black. Then the letters of these words disappear, and the secret message, in white, is revealed.

Chapter 4

Dangerous Missions

Some spies carry out covert ops (operations). These are illegal, dangerous, and sometimes deadly behind-the-scenes missions—and deadly missions call for deadly weapons. During the Cold War, secret agencies designed all sorts of secret weapons.

Some were guns disguised as everyday objects—a ball-point pen, a ring, a cigarette lighter. An East German female spy had a pistol in her purse disguised as a tube of lipstick. This lipstick pistol could fire a single shot. It was nicknamed the Kiss of Death.

From the outside, this pistol looks like a lipstick tube.

The Soviet Union sometimes sent agents to assassinate enemies. One weapon looked like a cigarette pack but was actually a gun that fired poison gas. Another was disguised as a cane. As the agent pressed the end against the victim and turned the cane clockwise, a needle shot out of the end and fired a fatal poison pellet into the victim.

An umbrella was used to kill Bulgarian Georgi Markov. Markov opposed Bulgaria's Communist government. He lived in London, England. Markov made anti-Communist statements on the radio. The Bulgarians and the Soviets didn't like what he said one bit.

One day in 1978, Markov was walking along a London street. He felt a small, sharp pain in his thigh. A man had just passed him by carrying an umbrella. Three days later, Markov was dead. He never knew that his assassin had pulled a trigger in the umbrella handle, sending a silent poison pellet into his thigh.

Georgi Markov (left) was murdered in 1978 with an umbrella that shot poison pellets (above).

Get Castro

Shortly after seizing power in 1959, Cuban president Fidel Castro set up a Communist government. Later, Castro made speeches criticizing the United States. Since Cuba is just 90 miles (145 km) from Florida, U.S. officials were worried.

In the 1960s, the CIA cooked up at least six secret plans to have Castro assassinated. Castro smokes lots of cigars, so agents thought about giving him poisoned cigars. Castro likes to swim in a certain spot off the Cuban coast, so agents looked into blowing him up with an exploding clamshell. He wears a diving suit when he swims, so they wanted to infect it with a harmful fungus.

Did agents put any of these wild plans into action? No one knows for sure. But if they ever did, the plans failed.

Cuban leader Fidel Castro (right) was an enemy of the CIA.

Tracking Down Ato

In the East African nation of Somalia, secret agents and U.S. Army forces used spy tech to pull off a daring plan. In 1993, a civil war raged in Somalia. Relief workers were handing out emergency food and medical supplies. U.S. troops protected the relief workers.

U.S. soldiers used spy tech to capture Osman Ato (above) in Somalia in 1993. Ato supplied weapons during a brutal civil war there.

CIA covert ops agents were there too. Their mission was to capture Osman Ato. He was an arms dealer who supplied the fighters with weapons. The United States hoped capturing Ato would help cool down the war and save lives.

The mission's key ingredient was a tiny electronic tracking device. CIA technicians hid the device in a walking stick. One of Ato's men agreed to help the CIA in exchange for money.

He met with Ato to give him the walking stick as a gift. Ato thanked him and drove off. U.S. Delta Force commandos followed the car in Blackhawk helicopters.

The soldiers kept their distance at first. They didn't worry about losing track of their target. The electronic device in the walking stick sent a constant stream of radio signals up to a satellite. It then beamed the

Blackhawk helicopters help with many U.S. secret missions.

information down to the commandos. The data showed up on global positioning system (GPS) receivers. It gave Ato's exact position in degrees of longitude and latitude.

When the time came to make a move, the soldiers flew the Blackhawks directly over Ato's car. A soldier leaned out and fired three rifle shots down into the car's engine.

The shots were perfectly placed. They knocked out the engine. The car stopped, and the Blackhawks hovered above. Then ropes dropped down, and commandos slid to the ground. Before Ato could react, he was hopelessly surrounded. The commandos quickly pulled Ato from the car, put him in handcuffs, and flew him away.

Escape from Iran

Not all covert operations use weapons. Some rely on disguises. Secret agents working in foreign countries often walk around disguised as ordinary citizens. Their disguise includes a cover, or false identity. If police question them, they can give a believable story for why they are there.

In November 1979, the Middle Eastern nation of Iran had a revolution. Overnight, rulers friendly to the United States were replaced by anti-U.S. rulers. Sixty-six U.S. government employees working in Iran were kidnapped and held hostage.

In the confusion, six other Americans escaped. They found hiding places in the capital city of Tehran. But they were stuck there. It was up to the CIA to get them out.

The Spy Dress Code

During the Cold War, Soviet secret agents had to follow a strict dress code. They were ordered not to dress like spies! That's because they operated undercover in countries such as France, Britain, and the United States. People in these nations had pictures in their heads of how spies ought to look, based on movies and TV shows. They pictured spies sneaking around in long trench coats, dark sunglasses, and a hat pulled down low. Or they imagined them in fancy tuxedos surrounded by beautiful women. Soviet spies were under strict orders to dress like ordinary people and never call attention to themselves.

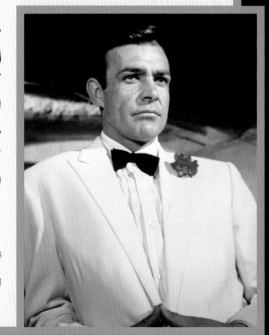

Many people in the United States and Europe expect spies to look like James Bond (right). Bond is a character in a series of action-filled spy movies.

CIA agent Antonio Mendez headed a covert operation to sneak the six Americans home. They would have to fly out from the Tehran airport, but the Iranians would arrest any Americans trying to leave the country. Iran still had friendly relations with Canada, though. So the six would be disguised as a Canadian movie crew working in Iran.

Mendez flew to Hollywood, California. He met with a movie makeup artist to discuss disguises. Meanwhile, CIA agents put together their fake identities. Besides Canadian passports, there were personal histories, including names and birth dates, to create. Everything had to seem true.

Antonio Mendez (below) worked as a CIA agent for twenty-five years. In 1979 he planned a difficult rescue of six Americans trapped in Iran.

These six Americans used disguises and other spy tricks to escape from Iran in 1980.

Mendez and another CIA agent arrived in Iran on January 25, 1980. They met secretly with the six Americans. All six memorized new names, birth dates, jobs, and personal histories.

Three days later, they were ready. They left for the airport in disguise. The wait at the airport was long and difficult, and the flight was delayed. Iranian authorities examined their passports and questioned them for hours. But in the end, Mendez's covert operation worked. The six Americans flew safely out of Iran and headed home.

chapter 5

Future Spy Tech

The Cold War ended in the early 1990s. The Soviet Union broke apart into fifteen smaller countries. The biggest of those countries is Russia. But Russia is no longer the focus of U.S. spying. U.S. intelligence agencies have shifted their attention to terrorism. They track down terrorists worldwide and try to prevent terrorist attacks at home.

This new focus calls for new spy technologies. Most terrorists fight in small groups and stage violent surprise attacks. For foot soldiers, wiping out terrorists often means house-to-house fighting in cities. Soldiers also may search mountainous areas for terrorist hiding spots.

Micro air vehicles (MAVs) could help soldiers. MAVs are spy planes of the future. These mini aircraft are light enough to be carried on a soldier's back. The U.S. Army has been testing one that flies like a helicopter. It's just 13 inches (33 centimeters) high and is powered by a gasoline engine.

These photos show tests of micro air vehicles (MAVs).

During its flight, the micro-copter beams back images to TV monitors in a nearby ground station, giving a moment-to-moment view of the scene below. Soldiers in the station can update ground troops by radio about the dangers that await them.

Robot Spies

Engineers are designing robots that act like insects and animals. They're creating flies, fish, lobsters, and more. These robot spies could go anywhere on Earth—or up in the air or underwater—to steal secrets.

The CIA built this robotic catfish in 1999. It's in the private CIA museum at the CIA headquarters in Langley, Virginia.

The key is the new science of biomimetics—imitating a real creature in robot form. A fly is a perfect example. Scientists ask how flies do the amazing things they do. They can take off and land in any direction, even upside down, and change direction in thirty-thousandths of a second.

Scientists look at a real fly as if it were a machine to find out how it works. This way of thinking is called reverse engineering—taking something apart to see how it works. Once engineers understand how the real thing works, they try making a robot that works the same way.

Robofly

Can people really make a robotic housefly? A team of biologists, engineers, and scientists in California is trying. They call the project Robofly.

Robofly is a work in progress. The team has been making new, improved versions since 2001. In one version, Robofly is smaller than a quarter and weighs less than a paper clip. It has polyester wings 0.5 inch (1.3 cm) long. The wings are about one-twentieth as thick as the page you are reading. This Robofly stands on solar panels that supply energy to a tiny motor. The motor flaps and rotates the wings 150 times a second, the speed of an actual fly.

This Robofly can flap its wings and almost take off, but it doesn't yet have enough power to fly. Once it can fly, it will need to navigate on its own without crashing into walls. One day, the team hopes to develop a computer control system to solve this problem. They also want to make a lightweight camera so that Robofly can gather IMINT as it flies.

This robotic fly may one day go on spy missions.

Terrorist Faces

Facial recognition is a new spy technology that may help fight terrorists. This tool is useful because no two people on Earth look exactly alike. Our eyes, noses, and mouths are all slightly different. Computer scientists are designing a software system to store the faces of known or suspected terrorists. The system is for use in public places.

Olympics Spies

For the 2004 Olympic Games in Athens, Greece, $1.5 billion was spent to guard against terrorist attacks. About seventy thousand security personnel patrolled the stadiums and surrounding streets. A blimp equipped with high-powered cameras gathered IMINT from above. On the street, spy vans cruised the streets. These precautions were expensive, but they worked. The games were a peaceful success.

This software has been tested in airports. When passengers pass through security gates, video cameras capture their faces. The software analyzes each face and converts the features into computer codes. If the codes match the codes of one of the terrorist faces in the database, the system signals a match, and airport security officials are warned.

In 2004, a British police force developed a computer system to compare security camera footage with photographs of known criminals.

Public Places

Terrorists often attack famous buildings. On September 11, 2001, terrorists hijacked four airplanes. One plane crashed into the Pentagon near Washington, D.C. Another crashed in a Pennsylvania field. The other two planes struck the World Trade Center in New York City.

A new spy tech tool known as the Synchronized Operations Command Complex (SOCC) is helping our government in Washington, D.C. That city is the home of famous structures such as the White House and the U.S. Capitol building. Dozens of cameras watch these potential terrorist targets and the streets around them twenty-four hours a day.

The heart of SOCC is a room with a wall of forty video screens. Each screen is fed by a surveillance camera. Police watch the screens and control the cameras. They can even zoom in on individual faces.

One day, police hope to link the surveillance cameras to facial recognition databases in the United States and around the world. Then any face caught on camera could be checked against faces of terrorists. SOCC and other new spy tools hold the promise of something we all look forward to—a safer and more secure world.

Am I Being Spied On?

Are you worried about people spying on you? You can buy a telephone debugger for as little as $100. This device keeps your phone conversations from being recorded. And what about hidden cameras? For just $80, you can buy a lipstick-sized detector. It sounds an alarm to warn you if any secret video cameras are watching.

Spy tech keeps playing bigger parts in our lives. Every day more of these devices are out there. And engineers and scientists are always at work making more of them.

Glossary

bug—a combination microphone-radio transmitter device for picking up conversations in secret

Central Intelligence Agency (CIA)—the U.S. secret agency responsible for spying on other nations

Cold War—the years between 1945 and 1991, when the United States and the Soviet Union constantly spied on each other

communications intelligence (COMINT)—intelligence in the form of messages, usually carried by radio waves

counterspying—making sure that spies from foreign nations don't steal your nation's secrets

covert operations—secret missions conducted by agents and soldiers, often aimed at capturing or killing enemies or rescuing hostages

Federal Bureau of Investigation (FBI)—U.S. secret agency that keeps foreign spies from stealing secrets in the United States. FBI agents also hunt for suspected terrorists and other kinds of criminals.

image intelligence (IMINT)—intelligence in the form of pictures

intelligence: information gathered by professional spies

KGB—Soviet secret agency responsible for spying during the Cold War

National Security Agency (NSA)—U.S. secret agency that analyzes intelligence gathered by other secret agencies. It also works to keep spies from other countries away from secret U.S. government information.

night vision devices (NVD)—cameras, goggles, and binoculars that make it possible to see in nearly total darkness

radio waves—invisible waves of energy that carry electrical signals, used to transmit radio and TV broadcasts and telephone and e-mail messages

silicon chip—small piece of silicon holding thousands of transistors for storing and transmitting electrical information. It is a key ingredient in computers.

sneakies—sneaky tools, such as bugs and minicameras, that spies use to gather intelligence

spy technology—tools that professional spies and law enforcement officers use to gather intelligence and track down criminals

surveillance—the ongoing observation of a person or group

Selected Bibliography

Gannon, James. *Stealing Secrets, Telling Lies: How Spies and Codebreakers Helped Shape the Twentieth Century.* Washington, DC: Brassey's, 2001.

Keefe, Patrick Radden. *Chatter: Dispatches from the Secret World of Global Eavesdropping.* New York: Random House, 2005.

Keegan, John. *Intelligence in War.* New York: Alfred Knopf, 2003.

Melton, H. Keith. *Ultimate Spy.* New York: Dorling Kindersley, 2002.

Richelson, Jeffrey T. *The Wizards of Langley.* Boulder, CO: Westview Press, 2001.

For quoted material: "Navajo Code Talkers," The Navajo Nation, 2005, http://www.navajo.org/history.htm (October 24, 2005).

Further Reading and Websites

Central Intelligence Agency Homepage for Kids. http://www.cia.gov/cia/ciakids/index_2.shtml. Besides information on the CIA, this site includes a section on famous movie and TV spies and the gadgets they used.

Fridell, Ron. *Spying: The Modern World of Espionage.* Brookfield, CT: Twenty-First Century Books, 2002. This book gives an in-depth look at spying since the Cold War.

International Spy Museum. http://www.spymuseum.org. This is the website of the International Spy Museum in Washington, D.C. It includes information about museum exhibits, special programs, and games.

NSA/CSS Kids and Youth Page. http://www.nsa.gov/kids/index.cfm. Test your skill at breaking codes and ciphers, and check out the games and puzzles at this site, run by the National Security Agency.

Owen, David. *Spies: The Undercover World of Secrets, Gadgets and Lies.* Richmond Hill, ONT: Firefly Books, 2004. This book tells the story of spy history and has a lot of information about famous spies.

Payment, Simone. *American Women Spies of World War II.* New York: Rosen, 2004. Find out how U.S. women helped win World War II.

Platt, Richard. *Spy.* New York: Dorling Kindersley Publishing, Inc., 1996. Take a look at some of the top secret gadgets spies once used.

Wiese, Jim. *Spy Science: 40 Secret-Sleuthing, Code-Cracking, Spy-Catching Activities for Kids.* New York: Wiley, 1996. Learn how to create your own disguise, build a periscope, and more.

Wikipedia List of Cryptography Topics. http://en.wikipedia.org/wiki/List_of_cryptography_topics. This page has links to dozens of articles on secret codes.

Index

Acoustic Kitty, 17
American Revolution, 24
animals as spies, 11, 17
Ato, Osman, 33

Blackhawk helicopters, 33–34
Bond, James, 35
Bosnia and Herzegovina, 12–13
Britain, 25–26
bugs (listening devices), 14–17, 18

cameras, 6–7, 8–9, 11, 15, 28–29, 43
Canadians, 16–17, 36–37
Castro, Fidel, 32
cell phones, 14, 20
China, 4
CIA, 7, 8, 11, 15, 17, 32, 33, 35–37, 40
ciphers, 22
codes, 22, 25
Cold War, 7, 9, 10, 15, 16, 29, 30, 35, 38
COMINT, 14–21
Communism, 7, 31
Cuba, 32
Czechoslovakia, 15

Discoverer 14, 11
disguises, 4, 34–37

Echelon, 20–21
e-mail, 14, 18–19, 20
Europe, 4–5, 12

facial recognition, 41–42, 43
FBI, 8, 18–19

Germany, 25–26
guns, 30

hockey, 16

IMINT, 6–13, 41
invisible ink, 27–28
Iran, 34–37
Iwo Jima, 25

Jefferson, Thomas, 23–24

KGB, 7

laser microphones, 5, 17
lipstick gun, 30–31
London, 31

Markov, Georgi, 31
mass graves, 13
Mendez, Antonio, 36–37
Mexico, 26
micro air vehicles (MAVs), 38–39
missiles, 9
missile sites, 5, 8, 29
Moscow, 16

Navajo language, 25
night vision cameras, 8–9
night vision devices (NVDs), 5, 7–9
NSA, 8, 21

Olympic Games, 42
Operation Pigeon, 11

photons, 8
pixels, 29
poison, 31
Polybius Square, 23
Powers, Francis Gary, 9–10
Predator, 10

radio waves, 14, 19–20

Robofly, 40–41
robotic animals, 39–41

satellites, 5, 10–13, 20–21, 33
secret containers, 26–27
secret weapons, 30–31
silicon chips, 12
silk, 4–5
silkworms, 4–5
sneakies, 6, 16, 26–27
Somalia, 32–34
Soviet Union, 7, 10, 16, 27, 31
spy planes, 9–10, 13

terrorism and terrorists, 18, 21, 38, 41–43
Texas, 19
Trenton, Battle of, 24

umbrella, 31
unmanned aerial vehicles (UAVs), 10
USA Patriot Act, 19
U.S. government, 7, 26
U-2 plane, 9, 13

Washington, D.C., 11, 43
Washington, George, 24
World War I, 9, 25–26
World War II, 6, 25, 26

Yemen, 10

Zimmerman Telegram, 25–26

Photo Acknowledgments

The images in this book are used with the permission of: © Royalty-Free/CORBIS, background photos on pp. 1, 2, 4, 6, 8, 10, 12, 14, 16, 18, 20, 22, 24, 26, 28, 30, 32, 34, 36, 38, 40, 42, 44, 46, 48; © SuperStock, Inc./SuperStock, p. 5; © TopFoto/Karl Prouse/National News/The Image Works, p. 6; Sgt. 1st Class Johancharles Van Boers/United States Department of Defense, p. 9; © USAF/Getty Images, p. 10 (top); AP/Wide World Photos, pp. 10 (bottom), 16, 31 (bottom), 33, 36, 40; © Boyer/Roger-Viollet/The Image Works, p. 11; Smithsonian National Air and Space Museum (SI 2006-2665), p. 12; © MAIMAN RICK/CORBIS SYGMA, p. 13; © Bettmann/CORBIS, pp. 14, 35, 37; International Spy Museum, pp. 15, 31 (top); © Erica Johnson/Independent Picture Service, p. 18; © age fotostock/SuperStock, p. 20; National Security Agency, p. 21; Monticello/Thomas Jefferson Foundation, Inc., p. 24; © Jeffrey L. Rotman/CORBIS, p. 26; © Mary Evans Picture Library/The Image Works, p. 27; © popperfoto.com, p. 28 (both); © Greg Mathieson/Rex Features USA, p. 30; © ADALBERTO ROQUE/AFP/Getty Images, p. 32; Defense Visual Information Center, pp. 34, 39 (right); Pfc. Kyndal Brewer/United States Department of Defense, p. 39 (top); Tech. Sgt. Paul Dean/Air Force News Agency/www.af.mil/news, p. 39 (bottom); R.S. Fearing/UC Berkeley, p. 41; PA/PA/EMPICS, p. 42.

Front cover: © Sam Lund/Independent Picture Service (top); Defense Visual Information Center (center); © Digital Art/CORBIS (bottom); © Royalty-Free/CORBIS (background). Back cover: © Royalty-Free/CORBIS.

About the Author

Ron Fridell has written for radio, television, and newspapers. He has also written books about the Human Genome Project and the use of DNA to solve crimes. In addition to writing books, Mr. Fridell regularly visits libraries and schools to conduct workshops on nonfiction writing. He lives in Tucson, Arizona.